THE AUTOBIOGRAPHY OF MARY FRANCIS:

Albany to Toledo

By

David Newsome, Jr.

Published by Lulu Press, Inc.

Introduction

Mary Francis Luton passed December 31, 2011, just three days from her 78th birthday, from causes, as stated on the death certificate, attributable to debility (and other factors) or, in layman's terms, and in my opinion, from being, quite simply, tired: tired of being in the hospital, the nursing home, and hospice; tired of living in tremendous pain from ill legs; tired of pain from a bedsore on her backside that went to her bone; tired of pain killers; tired of immobility, unable to do what she has been able to do her entire life; tired, well, of living.

This book is the result of Mary's dictating her life to me in person and via telephone, over about the span of a year or so, and very sporadically, on or about 2002. Admittedly, this book is extremely short. There is a tremendous amount of material missing, and scant details are presented for what is included. You see, Mary, although she had a copy of the first rough draft, could not find it within herself to actually finish editing it. She said it made her sad. However, the intent of both Mary and I was to simply provide a brief history of her early years for her offspring in Toledo. In this sense, I believe this book accomplishes its purpose, as many of the facts herein were unknown to me and are quite probably unknown to most of my Toledo relatives, unlike her life in her later years, which we all know quite well. Consider this book to be a start, an overall outline of Mary's life. I will continue to research family history, and print new revised editions to address previously unknown material, and the reader should feel free to submit me additional data, stories, etc., and I will try my utmost to incorporate them in future editions.

The writing style is mostly mine, although I've tried to stay true to Mary's language when I could. I apologize in advance if it's unclear. Mary Francis is gone, but with this book, as well as with the myriad of photos and, most importantly, with her life as an example, she will never be forgotten.

Her loving son,

David Newsome, Jr.

1.
Early Years and Background

Because I was coming out feet first, and because she had no experience with feet first deliveries, the midwife, who my grandparents hired to bring me into the world, panicked. She shouted to my grandfather that she just couldn't do it. My grandfather ran to Dr. Lucas's house, and Dr. Lucas told my grandfather to immediately take my mother to the hospital.

I was born on January 3, 1934, at 5:58 p.m. at Phoebe Putney Memorial Hospital in Albany, Georgia, to Ida Lee Luton. She was 15 years old at the time. On my birth certificate , an empty space occupies the box "Father." At that time, birth certificates also listed whether the child was legitimate or illegitimate. My box was checked "illegitimate," though my mother knew quite well who my father was, a one Robert Lee Roundtree.

My father, however, was never part of my life. He drowned in the Flint River in Albany when I was very young. From what I've been told, my father, who happened to be a good swimmer, was in a boat with some friends, drinking. The boat capsized and everyone was thrown out. My father made it to shore. But when he saw that two others wouldn't make it, he went back to save them. All three drowned.

I understand that it took three weeks to find his body. Because of the terrible condition it was in, my father's casket was closed at his funeral.

My mother was tall, slim — In fact, many people called her Slim — with a dark complexion. She had very long, black hair, of which my grandparents were quite proud. My grandparents thought she'd be the first of their children to graduate from high school. But after she had me, she never went back to school. I believe she made it to the 10th grade.

Louisa Luton and Sam Luton were my grandparents. Louisa, born in 1887, had a total of eight children, the first three by Will Smith and the last five by my grandfather, Sam, who was born in 1880. Will's children were Robert Smith, Mary Anne, and Francis Cotea.

Sam's children were Henry Lee, Essie Lee (1911), Howling Cherry (1909; I have no idea where my grandfather got this name. Howling Cherry later changed his name to Ollie), Carl Lee (1917), and my mother, Ida Lee (1919).

I never lived with my mother while I was growing up. My grandparents raised me. We lived at 706 Tiff Avenue from my birth until my grandfather died, when I about 12 years old. My mother also lived there, until she married Jim Willie, when I was very young.

The house on Tiff had three rooms. The kitchen was attached to the house but had its own entrance. The front door opened into the front bedroom where we slept. My grandparents had their bed and I had mine.

Both my grandparents worked. My grandmother washed white folks clothes; in particular, those of the Pace family. The Paces were nice white folks. My grandmother would walk to their house, pick up their clothes, and carry them home in a basket on her head. Some of my friends and I sometimes helped my grandmother wash and iron the clothes. I remember a girlfriend named Abbey, who helped us iron. One day, she accidentally dropped the smoothing iron on my leg.

I recall my grandfather working at a turpentine steel mill. He always seemed to be mending an open sore caused by hitting his leg with a hammer at the mill. It never healed completely. Once he could no longer work at the mill, he took a job out of town. I don't recall what exactly he did. I believe that his open sore probably was cancerous and ultimately killed him, because I don't recall his dying from anything in particular.

As I mentioned above, my mother stayed with my grandparents until she married Jim Willie. I recollect that he was a nice man, a little taller than my mother. They moved out of Albany and wanted to take me. My grandparents, however, did not want me to leave. They were concerned about how Jim Willie would treat me, since I wasn't his biological child. So, I stayed with my grandparents.

Although my father had died, I recall going over to the house of my father's mother, Grandma James. She and Aunt Sis were always happy to see me. I also recall a half sister named Henrietta Roundtree. She was about twelve years older than I was. She married Joe Hicks, who was the brother of one of my friends, Eula Hicks. Eula told me that they later divorced and that Henrietta moved to Chicago. That's the last I heard of them.

2.
Elementary School Years

I have fond memories of my early years living with my grandparents. They both were very loving and caring people who wanted nothing more than for me to be a success in life. Like most black folk at that time, my grandparents didn't have much of an education. My grandmother was fortunate enough to get to the sixth grade, but my grandfather didn't even make it that far. If he could read, it wasn't too well, as I recall my grandmother reading the newspaper to him while he listened attentively. Consequently, they really stressed my getting an education. My earliest school memories are my attending nursery school.

The nursery school was at the house of Mary Jane Ford, who was a teacher and member of our church. I don't recall much about her except that she had her first child in her forties, a son named him Preston Ford, after his father.

After nursery school, I attended the first grade at Tiff Elementary School, down the street from our house. There was no kindergarten at the time. Of course, this was before desegregation and the school was an all black school, with all black teachers and students.

Tiff actually consisted of two buildings. The first and second graders were housed in a little white building. The other building, about a half block away, housed grades two to seven. It was somewhat larger and was also white. Across the street were projects where some of my relatives lived.

I walked to Tiff. Sometimes, my grandfather would walk with me, and sometimes I'd walk with other children. I remember walking with the children of Georgia Ann, a neighbor, who had 15 children.

I still remember my first grade teacher, Ms. Gertrude. She was an older, light skinned lady with beautiful hair. She was a very sweet lady who really loved her students.

I always did well in school and I enjoyed school. I usually earned A's and B's and an occasional C.

My grandparents became Seventh-Day Adventist when I was six years old. We attended Albany Seventh Day Adventist Church. I was very active in the church early on. I sung in the choir, often solos, read the mission stories, and attended camp meetings.

I remember one family that was very active in the church, Dr. Parks and his wife, whose name I can't recall. At times, Dr. Parks was the only church member with a car. He was very caring and would ensure that everyone had a ride to church and back.

The Parks didn't have any children, but they took an active role in my life and that of my friend, Mildred Mathis. Dr. Park continuously told the two of us to stay in school and to go to college.

Two significant events happened when I was 12 and 14 years old.

When I twelve my grandfather died, in 1946, after which my grandmother and I moved into Aunt Cotie's house at 424 Corn Avenue in Albany. Aunt Cotie was concerned about the two of us living alone, so she moved us in with her.

I recall it being a one story, white house trimmed in green. It had four rooms and a kitchen. Mr. Chaplain, for whom Aunt Cotie cooked, built a bathroom onto the house. A plum tree was on one side of the yard and a pecan tree on the other.

When I was 14, my mother married again, for the second time, this time to Jesse Giles. Jessie was in the

Army, stationed at Turner Field Air Base. Over the years, my mother and Jesse Giles married and divorced each other at least twice. After Turner Air Base, they went to Fort McDill, Tampa, Florida. Then, my mother got ill and came home to stay with us at Aunt Cotie's house.

Once, my mother was really sick, and Aunt Cotie had a doctor examine my mother. The doctor said that my mother had a seven pound tumor in her stomach, and he wanted to operate that following Monday.

Aunt Cotie didn't believe his diagnosis and had another doctor look at her. He said she'd be okay and told my Aunt that she would call him shortly and, when she did, he'd tell her what to do. Well, Ms. Odella, our next door neighbor, was over then. My mother asked Ms. Odella to help my mother to the pot, which she did. When my mother was using the pot, a baby came out of her.

Ms. Odella and I screamed and ran out of the house. After we went back into the house, my mother said she had to use the pot again. Another baby came out. My aunt called the doctor, as he said she would. He had known that my mother was pregnant and that the babies were dead. The doctor told my Aunt to get a cigar box, put the twins in it, dig a whole in the backyard, and bury them. And that's exactly what she did. I got up the nerve to look at the two dead twins. All I can remember is that they looked like flesh with hair. This was my mother's first set of twins. She would have two more sets. After she was well again, she went back to her husband in Tampa.

My mother then moved to Dayton, Ohio. I suspect that Giles was transferred to Wright Patterson Air Force Base. I believe that my mother and Giles divorced in Dayton.

My other aunts — Essie and Maryanne — then moved up to Dayton with my mother. My grandmother and I took the train, the L&M train, to Dayton to visit everyone. I liked the train ride. We'd only have to transfer once, in Cincinnati. The train station in Cincinnati was quite nice.

After the first trip, we would visit them every summer. My grandmother hated cold weather and snow, so she never wanted to stay in Dayton late in the year.

3.
High School Years

I attended Monroe High School from the 8th to 11th grade. Back then, high school didn't go to the 12th grade. My grandmother and I still lived with Aunt Cotie on Corn Avenue.

I have fond memories of my high school years. I sang in the high school choir throughout high school. The choir competed in numerous competitions and often won first place. We sang mostly gospel songs, which fit nicely with my participation in the church choir. I still remember singing "Great and Marvelous," and "The Heavens are Telling the Glory of God."

Elizabeth, whose last name I can't recall, was my best friend throughout high school. She was our class Valedictorian. She moved to Philadelphia shortly after graduation and I never heard from her again.

Sometime during high school, my grandmother sent me downtown to pay the last cataract payment to Dr. Irving. The elevator operator of the building, an elderly white man, said, when I got on the elevator, "Grandma, which floor?" Despite the fact that I was no older than 16, he called me "grandma." Many whites did that, and

I always thought it strange and resented it. Well, on this particular day, I didn't want to be called such, and I said to him, "Take ya momma up," and ran up the steps. I told Dr. Irving about it. With me in tow, he asked the elevator operator, "How old does she look to you?" He stuttered and said, "About 13, sir." To which Dr. Irving replied, "So why did you call her grandma?" Well, he turned beet red and apologized. Dr. Irving taught me a valuable lesson: Not all southern whites were racist. Some, like the good doctor, were really good people.

I graduated from Monroe High School May 25, 1950. I was 16 years old. My graduation was a big event because I was only the second one to graduate. My cousin Arnez, Aunt Essie's daughter, was the first to graduate from high school. At this time, they had already moved to Dayton. There, my mother, Aunts Essie and Maryanne had made a reputation for themselves as cooks. They worked in Swelles, an upscale restaurant in downtown Dayton. They were known as the three sisters. My mother was primarily responsible for salads, Aunt Assie for pies, and Aunt Maryanne cakes, but they all chipped in on all of the cooking. Anyway, Aunts Essie and

Maryanne came down for my graduation, and all of the local relatives attended as well. I don't recall my mother being there.

4.
College Years

After graduating from high school, I became the first member of my immediate family to attend college. I enrolled into Albany State College. I always wanted to be a teacher and so I majored in education. I was 16. The college was, of course, an all black college, and was the closest college to my neighborhood. It was within walking distance of Aunt Cotie's house.

Professor Summons was my biology teacher at Albany State. He actually knew my grandmother. When he attended Albany State, before I was born, my grandmother would pack his lunch and give him some money. He told the class this, and that he would not let me fail because of the kindness my grandmother showed to him.

One day, Mildred, a close friend of mine, and I stopped at Kressage Five and Dime Store. This was long before Rosa Parks and the Civil Rights Movement. Well, we wanted some ice cream. Two young white women were working the ice cream counter. Mildred and I waited until all the whites had been served and we were next in line. But, instead of serving us, the two white girls laughed at us and waited until other whites wanted something and served them. Well, a white man confronted the girls and told them to serve us. To get even, we ordered fifty cents worth of candy and, after they got it for us, we told them to take eat it themselves and ran out of the store.

The time was the early 50s and black folks were tired of segregation and the whole second class citizen thing. It was during the time that Blacks automatically sat in the back of the bus. If the bus got too crowded, the blacks moved even out of the black seats. If the bus was so crowded that someone had to get off, it was always a black person who got off.

I only attended Albany State for one year. Around 1951, when I was seventeen, my grandmother wanted me to leave Albany and go to Dayton. She thought I could get a better education and have a better life up North. My grandmother was also scared for me, as times were changing. She thought I was too outspoken around white folk and that it would lead to trouble.

5.
Dayton, Ohio

So, did I go up North? Not at all. I left Albany and enrolled in Oakwood College in Huntsville, Alabama, located even deeper in the South. Oakwood was a Seventh-Day Adventist college and I had been an Adventist for most of my life, so it was a natural fit. However, I was only there one semester when my mother got sick again, around January, 1952.

She was living in Dayton, with the rest of her sisters. I left school and went to Dayton. I didn't have a place of my own and stayed with my mother or Aunt Essie. I didn't stay all the time with my mother because she liked to drink and have a good time. So, I often stayed with my Aunts, who were more involved in the church.

My mother's sickness was due to her pregnancy, and she was again pregnant with twins. At this time, she and Giles were divorced so I don't know if Giles was the father. Like her first set, her second set of twins were also stillborn.

Twins ran in the family. I was living with my mother on 5th Street when she got pregnant again, and again she was pregnant with twins —

for a third time. The last time was a charm and on May 8, 1954, she gave birth at Miami Valley Hospital to two boys, Larry and Terry, both premature and about four pounds each. Larry was the weaker twin and almost died. He was born with asthma.

My mother kept Giles as her last name, so my brothers were Larry and Terry Giles, although Giles was not their father. I don't recall the name of their father, but I remember that he was an older man, medium height, dark complexioned with a little gray in his hair. He used to come to the house a few times.

When Larry was fourteen months he got spinal meningitis. (Larry was in the hospital quite often until about five years old, when he seemed to outgrow his illnesses).

At this time, my mother told us that she had breast cancer. She had had it for a while, but just didn't tell us about it. In 1956, my mother had her left breast removed at Miami Valley Hospital. Years later the cancer would reoccur. I remember that those were very trying and sad times.

I held different, odd jobs, and attended business school for about six months, but I dropped out. I got really involved in the Ethan Temple Church on William Street. I held numerous positions in the youth ministry.

I met Ernest when I lived on 5th Street with my mother. He lived next door to us with Rose, a good friend the family. I was about 21 years old and he was about 28. Ernest and I started dating, and had an on and off again relationship. One thing led to another, and we ended up with three children, Pam, who was born in April 22, 1955, and my first set of twins, Marlene and Darlene Roundtree, born in 1957. Pam was born at Miami Valley Hospital, and the twins at St. Elizabeth Hospital.

I got really sick while pregnant with the twins. I think it was because I had to take care of my mother and my brothers, Larry and Terry. I stopped going to my medical appointments because of this. In fact, I didn't know I was having twins until near their birth.

Ernest was still around, but we really had no relationship to speak of. He worked but didn't make much. I took him to court for child support. He told the judge that he was only making about 45 dollars a week, and that you can't' get blood out of a turnip. To which the judge said, "You're right. I've never heard of anyone getting blood out of a turnip. But you can jail the turnip." The people in the courtroom burst out laughing. That was all Ernest needed and he paid child support from then on.

Ernest and I never married, although we planned it a couple of times. He changed his mind once and I changed mine once. I was reluctant to marry him because he was a player, a ladies man.

I had my second set of twins, Greta and Gretchen, on June 3, 1960. I just knew that after Marlene and Darlene, I would not have another set of twins. I just couldn't believe it when I found out I would have another set. It was the fifth set of twins between my mother and me.

Their father was James Johnson. He was stationed at Wright Patterson Air Base. A friend of mine introduced us. Our relationship didn't last too long. I didn't have much contact with him, and he never saw the twins.

From 5th Street, my mother and I moved into a duplex on Westwood Street. That's where I met David Newsome. I wasn't dating Ernest or anyone else at the time. I took Larry and Terry to a barbershop on 5th Street where Dave was a barber. Dave was thin, about six feet tall, with short hair.

Dave had met my mother earlier and knew that she was sick. He told me that there was no need coming by the barbershop, and that he would come to the house to cut Larry and Terry's hair. That when we started dating.

When I met Dave, he was married, but he and his wife were separated. They were from Patterson, Mississippi, and had four children, all girls. Dave would often bring the girls to the house with him.

My mother, Ida Lee Giles, died on Easter, April 22, 1962, from complications of cancer. She was only 43 years old. I was devastated.

At this time, I was pregnant. Dave and I had two boys, David and Darryl. Dr. Washington delivered David on June 25, 1962. David was named after his father and was his father's first son.

Darryl was born on August 30, 1964 when we lived on Woodward Street. David was in jail at the time for not paying child support to his ex-wife. Dave and his ex-wife had a very difficult relationship.

After Dave and his wife divorced, he and I married at my house in a small ceremony on Cooper Street in 1966. I had custody of Larry and

Terry at that time, and seven children of my own.

6.
The Toledo Years

Dave was always a traveling man. I would get a call from him, saying "I'm in Cleveland." Or, he'd just up and visit his relatives in Chicago or Mississippi. He'd often call me after he arrived, without informing me in advance of his plans. He'd drive whatever piece of car he had at the time, and not too infrequently, he'd call me from someplace to tell me that he was catching the bus. He visited Toledo, Ohio a few times and decided he wanted to live there.

In Toledo, he met Reverend Robinson and Brother Waddell. They wanted him to start a church in Toledo. Dave often preached and had religious services at the house. So, we decided to move to Toledo, which we did in 1966.

We first lived across the street from Lincoln School, on Lincoln Street. Dave had arrived in advance and gotten a job as a barber at Clark's Barbershop on Detroit Street. He sent for me and told me that the house was ready. Well, when we arrived, the house was still being worked on. So I told Dave that we couldn't stay in an incomplete house. We only stayed there a few weeks before we moved again.

Dave met Mr. Ovel Wright, who had a house on Brand, off Detroit Avenue, that he rented to us.

Pam was in the 7th Grade and Marlene and Darlene the 5th. We later moved to Yondota street on the East Side. All the children, except Pam, went to Navarre Elementary School, down the street. Pam was in high school and attended Waite High School. I went to school for nurse's aide for about six months. While I was in school, Dave would watch the children or I would get a babysitter.

When we lived on Yondota Street, Dave was again arrested on a warrant for not paying child support. He had to serve time in the Dayton workhouse. I took the children to visit him one time. I was shocked. He had had a mental breakdown. He seemed totally different. He was on medication and it made him very mellow. He walked really slowly. After his release from the workhouse, he came back to Toledo.

We lived on Yondota Street for four years. Then we moved into a house on Bronson street, but only stayed there one year before moving into a Metropolitan Housing Authority house on 736 Bronson Street in 1970. There was a very long waiting list to get into the Pulley Homes. When we went to apply, the lady that interviewed us said that Dave had a very impressive service record. Shortly after the interview, we got the house. We ended up living on Bronson for 23 years, longer than any other place I had ever lived.

While on Bronson, I worked as a private duty nurse for various people. Dave worked at a factory, but he continued to barber.

At the age of 40, I had Derrick, my last child. It was a difficult pregnancy because at my age.

I went back to school, enrolling into a new program called New Careers, a program designed for middle-aged people who wanted to start a new career. I was accepted by the Toledo Board of Mental Retardation, and I did social work. I graduated in 1979 with an Associate Degree in Social Work.

Conclusion

There. Was it not a quick read? I hope you found it interesting and, to some extent, enjoyable. And you make have learned a few things as well. As I mentioned previously, this is just the beginning. If you have any stories, facts, or anecdotes that you believe would further develop Mary's story, please don't hesitate to contact me at newsod@yahoo.com. Enjoy the pictures below. I apologize for the limited number of photos, but I don't have too many photos of Mary taken throughout her lifetime. Please feel free to send me any you think should be included in this book.

Sincerely,

David Newsome, Jr.

Mary's grandmother, Louisa Luton, date unknown.

Mary at the funeral of David Newsome, Sr., June 2000, in Dayton, Ohio.

Mary Francis and David Newsome, Jr., date unknown.

www.ingramcontent.com/pod-product-compliance
Ingram Content Group UK Ltd.
Pitfield, Milton Keynes, MK11 3LW, UK
UKHW020227250726
13967UKWH00001B/235

9 781105 536410